D1128675

DISCARD

Choosing a Hamster, Gerbil, Guinea Pig, Rabbit, Ferret, Mouse, or Rat

THE AMERICAN HUMANE ASSOCIATION
Pet Care Series

How to Choose and Care for a Small Mammal

Laura S. Jeffrey

Enslow Elementary
an imprint of
Enslow Publishers, Inc.
40 Industrial Road
Box 398
Berkeley Heights, NJ 07922
USA

http://www.enslow.com

American Humane Association™
The nation's voice for the protection of children & animals™

American Humane Association™
The nation's voice for the protection of children & animals™

Since 1877, American Humane Association has been at the forefront of virtually every major advance in protecting children, pets, and farm animals from cruelty, abuse, and neglect. Today we're also leading the way in understanding the human-animal bond and its role in therapy, medicine, and society. American Humane Association reaches millions of people every day through groundbreaking research, education, training, and services that span a wide network of organizations, agencies, and businesses. You can help make a difference, too. Visit www.americanhumane.org today, call 1-866-242-1877, or write to American Humane Association at 1400 16th Street NW, Suite 360, Washington, DC 20036.

To Our Readers: We have done our best to make sure all Internet addresses in this book were active and appropriate when we went to press. However, the author and the publisher have no control over and assume no liability for the material available on those Internet sites or on other Web sites they may link to. Any comments or suggestions can be sent by e-mail to comments@enslow.com or to the address on the back cover.

Every effort has been made to locate all copyright holders of material used in this book. If any errors or omissions have occurred, corrections will be made in future editions of this book.

♻ Enslow Publishers, Inc., is committed to printing our books on recycled paper. The paper in every book contains 10% to 30% post-consumer waste (PCW). The cover board on the outside of each book contains 100% PCW. Our goal is to do our part to help young people and the environment too!

Enslow Elementary, an imprint of Enslow Publishers, Inc.

Enslow Elementary® is a registered trademark of Enslow Publishers, Inc.

Copyright © 2013 by Enslow Publishers, Inc.

All rights reserved.

No part of this book may be reproduced by any means without the written permission of the publisher.

Library of Congress Cataloging-in-Publication Data

Jeffrey, Laura S.
  Choosing a hamster, gerbil, guinea pig, rabbit, ferret, mouse, or rat : how to choose and care for a small mammal / Laura S. Jeffrey.
    p. cm.—(The american humane association pet care series)
  Includes bibliographical references and index.
  Summary: "Discusses the selection, housing, diet, handling, grooming, and health of a new hamster, gerbil, guinea pig, rabbit, ferret, mouse, or rat"—Provided by publisher.
  ISBN 978-0-7660-4082-3
  1. Pets—Juvenile literature. 2. Mammals—Juvenile literature. I. Title.
  SF416.2.J458 2013
  636.088'7—dc23
                                 2011049144

Future Editions:
Paperback ISBN 978-1-4644-0217-3
ePUB ISBN 978-1-4645-1130-1
PDF ISBN 978-1-4646-1130-8

Printed in the United States of America
082012 Lake Book Manufacturing, Inc., Melrose Park, IL

10 9 8 7 6 5 4 3 2 1

Photo Credits: Adrin Shamsudin/Photos.com, p. 35; Artyom Rudenko/Photos.com, p. 42; Brock Fowler/Photos.com, p. 11; Cathy Keifer/Photos.com, p. 6; Duncan Noakes/Photos.com, p. 21; Eric Isselée/Photos.com, pp. 7, 16, 17 (bottom), 18; Erik Zunec/Photos.com, p. 30; Evgeniya Litovchenko/Photos.com, p. 37; Igor Dutina/Photos.com, p. 33; Josef Muellek/Photos.com, p. 43; Jupiterimages/Photos.com, p. 27; Matt Staples/Photos.com, p. 23; Shutterstock.com, pp. 4, 5, 8, 9, 10, 12, 13, 14, 15, 17 (top), 19, 20, 24, 32, 34, 36, 38, 39, 44, 45; Thinkstock/Photos.com, p. 40.

Cover Photo: Shutterstock.com (brown gerbil).

Table of Contents

R0440249436

Chapter 1
Great Pets

Small mammals, such as mice, rats, hamsters, gerbils, guinea pigs, rabbits, and ferrets, make great pets. Unlike cats and dogs, small mammals can fit into almost any room in any house. They do not need constant attention, so they are good pets for families who are often away during the day.

This is a ferret.

Rabbits are just one kind of small mammal.

Great Pets

This book will help you choose the right small mammal for you. It will tell you what to feed your new pet and how to make it feel comfortable and safe. You will learn how to keep your new pet healthy and happy.

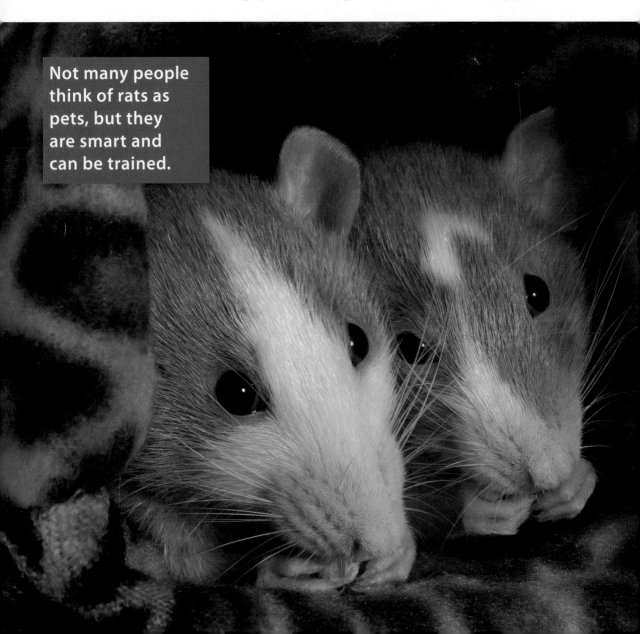

Not many people think of rats as pets, but they are smart and can be trained.

Chapter 2
The History of Small Mammals

Compared with other animals, small mammals do not have a long history as pets. For example, dogs and cats have been pets for thousands of years. But it was really not until the twentieth century that small mammals became household pets. Hamsters came to the United States in 1938. Before that time, they were used in Israel, France, and England for medical research.

A hamster

Ferrets are becoming popular pets. Find out if they are legal in your area before getting one.

Rabbits are believed to be the third most common pet in the United States.

Small mammals have become very popular pets. In fact, rabbits are believed to be the most common pet today after cats and dogs.

Ferrets are also becoming popular pets. In some areas, however, they are illegal. Or, you may need a license to have a ferret. Before bringing a ferret into your home, call your local wildlife department, fish and game department, or animal welfare agency. Find out if you are allowed to keep a ferret as a pet.

Chapter 3
The Right Pet for You

There are many different kinds of small mammals. You can choose to adopt a hamster, gerbil, guinea pig, ferret, rabbit, mouse, or rat. Each type of small mammal has its own needs, and each behaves in a certain way. It is important to pick a pet that matches your lifestyle.

Is a rat right for you?

Each type of small mammal needs special care and attention. Hamsters like to play with toys made just for them, such as this exercise wheel.

Mice and Rats

Many people are surprised to learn that mice and rats make terrific pets. Mice that are handled regularly become very gentle. Rats are very smart. They can be taught to respond to their owner's voice and touch. They also respond to food rewards.

With regular handling and care, mice and rats can become very gentle

Hamsters

Hamsters are clean and odorless. But they like to sleep during the day and stay up all night. They are also known to get upset easily, and they may bite or nip at their owners. Because of this, hamsters may not be the best small mammal for you.

Gerbils

Gerbils are gentle and curious. They become lonely when they are not around other gerbils. In some areas, gerbils are illegal. If you choose this small mammal, you should get two. Just make sure the two you choose are both male or both female.

Make sure gerbils are legal where you live before you decide to keep them as pets.

Guinea pigs come in many different colors.

Guinea Pigs

A guinea pig is also known as a cavy (rhymes with navy). They come in many breeds and colors. The three basic types are shorthaired, longhaired, and medium-length or swirl-coated. Guinea pigs learn to recognize their owners. They will greet a favorite person with loud whistles and squeaks. They are very social animals, so if you have room, get two.

Rabbits

Rabbits also come in many breeds. They are loyal, affectionate pets. They are also very playful and enjoyable to be around.

14

Ferrets

Many people find ferrets to be lovable pets. Ferrets have a lot of energy and are curious. Owners must be willing to pay extra time and attention to this pet. Ferrets are very social animals. They may get along well in houses with dogs and cats. Ferrets are smart and can even be trained to do tricks.

Ferrets make unique and interesting pets.

Learn More

You can learn more about the different kinds of small mammals by exploring Web sites on the Internet or visiting your local library. You can also call a humane society to get more information.

Once you have decided which small mammal to get, check with your local animal welfare agency. They may have small mammals that you could adopt. If they do not, ask your veterinarian to give you the name of a good breeder. A vet may also know people who are looking to find a new home for their own pets. Do not get your new pet from the wild. Wild animals do not make good pets.

Wherever you go to get your new pet, take your time and look around. The cage and the animal should be clean. The animal should be active and alert. If it is asleep, ask to have it awakened. Then, watch the animal move around and how it responds to you.

Fast Fact

A rat can be trained with food to come when its name is called.

The Right Pet for You

Fast Fact

If you are allergic to cats or dogs, you may be allergic to rabbits and guinea pigs, too.

The animal should not show any signs of poor health. These signs include not moving around, sneezing, scratching, discharge from the eyes or nose, bald spots, untreated injuries, a soiled area on or under the tail, or soft feces, or poop.

Animals should not have parasites, such as ear mites, worms, and maggots. Check the animal's bedding or droppings for parasites, too. Make sure the animal does not have crusty spots on the inside of its ears.

Many people who are allergic to cats and dogs are also allergic to rabbits and guinea pigs. These small mammals can shed heavily during certain times of the year. You may want to be tested for allergies before bringing any small mammal into your home.

When you get your new pet, check to make sure its coat is shiny and healthy.

Chapter 4

Taking Care of Your New Pet

A gerbil

No matter which small mammal you choose, set up its housing before you bring it home. The housing should be the proper size for your new pet. Avoid placing the housing in direct sunlight or in drafty areas. Your animal's house should be in its own quiet area of your home. Make sure the housing is secure. Avoid plastic housings because they can be chewed and your pet might escape.

The floor of the cage should be covered with solid flooring so your pet will not hurt its feet.

Mice and Rats

Mice and rats can be housed in either a big glass aquarium with a screened top or a solid-bottom cage with a wire top. To prevent any injuries to your pet's feet, make sure that most of the bottom of the cage is covered with solid flooring.

Taking Care of Your New Pet

Because rats are so smart, they usually will find a way out of their cage unless you secure it properly. If you have a wire cage, make sure the openings are not wide enough for your rat to squeeze through. The screened top should be weighted.

Inside the cage, put in ladders, tunnels, and safe toys for your pet to explore and enjoy. You should also add a fully enclosed nesting box. This box should be about five inches square with a small entrance. The entrance should be one inch for mice and two inches for rats. This nesting box can be as simple as a cardboard box. When the box becomes chewed or soiled, replace it.

Always place a few pieces of hardwood in the cage. Gnawing on the hardwood will help your pet wear down its always growing teeth.

Fast Fact

The teeth of all small mammals grow continuously. Your pet needs an unpainted and untreated piece of hardwood to chew on so it can keep its teeth short.

Taking Care of Your New Pet

The floor of the cage should be covered with shredded newspaper, kitty litter, peat moss, hay, or straw. This layer should be at least one inch deep so your pet can burrow, or dig a hole or tunnel and hide. Mice and rats are very curious, so give them toys. They like to explore boxes and chew on and crawl through cardboard tubes. Avoid wire exercise wheels because they pinch tails. A solid plastic wheel or runabout ball is a safer choice.

Use a water bottle that is the right size for your pet. Change the water daily. Feed your mice or rats special food made just for them. You can occasionally treat your mouse or rat to dried fruit slices, nuts, seeds, fiesta-type mixes, crackers, rolled oats, plain croutons, alfalfa hay, fresh fruits, dry cooked rice, and raisins. Remove any uneaten or spoiled food, or your pet may want to hoard it.

Your mouse or rat may enjoy raisins and nuts as treats. Do not feed cheese to any small mammals. It can make them sick.

Hamsters

A big glass aquarium with a screened top or a solid-bottom cage with a wire top is also a good home for a hamster. Unlike many animals, adult hamsters do not like company. They like to live alone, so keep only one hamster. Adult hamsters have been known to hurt or even kill their roommates.

Hamsters are also known for escaping from their cages. If this happens, place your pet's cage in the middle of the room with the door open and fresh food inside. In the morning, you may find that the hamster returned during the night and is now sleeping happily.

For bedding, hamsters prefer shredded paper, cat litter, peat moss, hay, or straw. You should also give them chew sticks and a nesting box.

Hamsters enjoy special hamster food. Feed your pet in the evening, and sometimes add vegetables or other fresh foods. Hamsters love to burrow. Hamsters are also hoarders, filling their cheek pouches with food and then scurrying away to hide their treasure.

Gerbils

Gerbils need a cage with plenty of room to burrow, nest, exercise, and leap. Buy a cage with lots of shelves, levels, and connecting tunnels. Give your pet lots of toys, such as paper rolls, branches, and cardboard boxes. Cover the floor of the cage with a thick layer of paper, which your pet will love to shred. You can also use unscented cat litter or sand.

Like hamsters, gerbils burrow. They also thump. For unknown reasons, every few days, gerbils go to a corner of their cage and thump their hind limbs. They are also great leapers and have earned the nickname "kangaroo rats." So make sure to securely cover the top of the cage.

Feed your gerbils specially prepared food mixture in the evening, when your pets are more active. Occasionally, treat your pets to dates, carrots, or alfalfa.

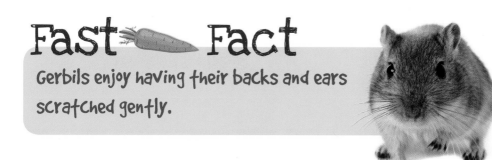

Fast Fact

Gerbils enjoy having their backs and ears scratched gently.

23

Guinea pigs need to be groomed. Their nails also need to be trimmed every few weeks.

Guinea Pigs

An ideal home for a guinea pig is a galvanized wire cage. It needs to have plenty of room for the guinea pig to burrow, nest, exercise, and leap. Cover the bottom of the cage with a sturdy carpet scrap or other solid flooring that can be easily replaced.

The best type of bedding for guinea pigs is a layer of hay or straw on top of a layer of peat moss. Hardwood blocks, such as chew toys, help wear down their teeth.

Guinea pigs eat often, so give them plenty of specially prepared guinea pig pellets. They also enjoy "greens," such as carrots, apples, timothy hay, and even fresh slices of orange. Do not give rabbit pellets to your guinea pig. Rabbit food does not have vitamin C, which a guinea pig needs.

Guinea pigs need to be groomed. They also have long nails that must be carefully trimmed every few weeks. Ask your veterinarian for help with this delicate task.

Guinea pigs need lots of room for exercise, or they will become obese. If possible, let your pet out of its cage in a closed room.

Rabbits

The best home for a rabbit is a galvanized wire cage made especially for rabbits. The cage should be at least four times bigger than the size of the rabbit. If you are getting a young rabbit, make sure the cage will be four times larger than the rabbit when it is fully grown. Partially cover the cage floor with cardboard or a sisal mat.

For bedding in the cage, place a thick layer of hay or straw on top of a layer of peat moss. Do not use sawdust because the dust can harm the rabbit's breathing system. Give your rabbit an enclosed sleeping box. The entrance should be at the top of one side.

You should not house your rabbit outside. Outdoor housing attracts flies that can make your rabbit sick. Outdoor rabbits may get heat stress in the summer and frostbite in the winter. Also, the rabbit's water might freeze in the winter. Your rabbit could also be attacked by other animals.

Rabbits need regular, supervised exercise outside their cages to stay healthy. Make sure your pet does not chew on electrical cords during its indoor outings.

Make sure your rabbit's cage will be big enough when it is fully grown.

Taking Care of Your New Pet

Unlike many other small mammals, a rabbit should have the chance to spend much of its awake time out of the cage. Rabbits require a larger area to exercise and play in.

The best diet for your rabbit is rabbit pellets. You can also give your rabbit alfalfa hay and a salt block. Some fresh vegetables can make your rabbit ill, so check with a vet or other expert for advice. Rabbits need fresh water, which should be changed every day. Rabbits can sometimes misbehave, so make sure the food and water bowls are too heavy for your pet to knock over.

Some people train their rabbits to use a litter box. They also let their pet roam inside—after rabbit-proofing the home, of course. Make sure no loose dogs, cats, or other pets will threaten the safety of your rabbit.

Pay special attention to your rabbit's toenails. They may need to be trimmed by a veterinarian because they grow rapidly. To prevent overgrown teeth, give your rabbit hay, straw, and blocks made of hardwoods to chew.

To avoid behavioral and health problems, pet rabbits should be spayed or neutered. If you get your rabbit from an animal shelter or rescue agency, this may have already been done for you.

Ferrets

Ferrets should be housed in cages large enough to hold a litter box, nesting and sleeping area, and toys. This usually amounts to a space that is at least fourteen inches wide by twenty-four inches long and ten inches high. Ferrets do not like temperatures above 95 degrees Fahrenheit, so do not place their cage in direct sunlight.

For nesting and sleeping, ferrets enjoy a soft cloth, old T-shirt, or a towel, which should be placed in the opposite corner from the litter box. When giving your ferret toys, keep in mind that you should not give it anything it can swallow.

Ferrets are carnivores, or meat eaters. They enjoy a diet of specially prepared food or cat food that is high in animal protein. Avoid feeding your ferret any dairy or sugar products. They can be harmful. Young ferrets, called kits, and old ferrets need special diets. Kits should be fed a cup of food a day that has been soaked in water for ten or fifteen minutes. Older ferrets have problems digesting the protein in their food, so you should add 1/2 teaspoon of vegetable oil to it.

Ferrets must eat a protein-rich diet.

Because ferrets have a lot of energy and are smart, be sure their food dishes are weighted so they cannot be tipped over. Also, be sure to place these dishes near the nesting area and not their litter box.

You should also let your ferret roam outside its cage regularly. Ferrets have a lot of energy and need to run and explore outside the cage every day. Just make sure to supervise your pet to keep it safe and to prevent it from becoming destructive.

Taking Care of Your New Pet

Your ferret will sometimes need a bath and nail trimming. Use a tearless baby shampoo or one made just for ferrets. Your ferret will need to be bathed only once every few months. Bathing it too much can bother a ferret's skin and cause its coat to become dull.

Ferrets, like dogs and cats, will need vaccinations and should be spayed or neutered to avoid health and behavior problems.

Things to Know

No matter which kind of small mammal you choose as a pet, make sure you clean its cage regularly. Every week, wash the entire cage with hot, soapy water. Use only liquid dishwashing soap. Rinse the cage and then dry it well before putting your pet back. After the cage is clean and dry, replace your pet's bedding. Do not use wood shavings, such as pine and cedar. They contain chemicals that can harm your pet.

All cage equipment, such as water bottles and food bowls, should be cleaned with watered-down bleach (for example, one tablespoon of bleach in one gallon of water) once a week. This stops bacteria buildup.

Taking Care of Your New Pet

If you are training your pet to use a litter box, do not use clay, clumping sand, cat litter, or corncob litters. These are harmful to small animals if swallowed. Instead, use plain (without print or ink) paper pulp, dry grass pellets, aspen wood shavings, or compressed sawdust pellets.

Always wash your hands before handling your pet. You may have traces of food, salt, or sugar on your skin that may cause the animal to bite. Make sure to wash your hands afterward as well.

No matter which small mammal you get for a pet, take good care of it.

Chapter 5
Healthy and Happy

A veterinarian is a doctor who takes care of sick and injured animals. A vet also makes sure animals stay healthy. There are no vaccinations for most small mammals. But a vet will be able to tell you if your pet is in good health. You may even want to take a small mammal to the vet for a checkup before you decide to take it home. A vet can also answer any questions you might have.

A guinea pig

A vet will make sure your small mammal stays healthy.

If your pet stops eating or drinking or is less active than normal, call the vet. You should also call if your pet is having trouble breathing, is not having bowel movements or is having diarrhea, or is having problems performing simple tasks.

Ferrets do need annual visits to the vet. They should get a checkup and a shot called a distemper booster. Distemper is a disease. The booster gives your pet extra protection against the disease. Ferrets, especially females, are likely to get tumors (growths) and stomach ulcers (sores). Watch your ferret's behavior. Call the vet right away if your ferret acts lethargic, which means it does not seem to have any energy. Also call the vet if your pet is not eating or drinking.

Fast Fact

To keep your pet healthy, feed it the correct food, make sure it has clean water, and clean its cage regularly.

Chapter 6

Preventing Problems

A ferret

Most small mammals bite if they are frightened or angry. So you should get your pet comfortable with being held. To pick up your mouse or rat, gently close your hand around it. Lift it by the base of the tail with one hand while slipping your other hand under its body. Never squeeze or pick up a mouse or rat by the tail, midsection, or base of the neck.

Learn the proper way to pick up your new pet.

Be gentle when handling your hamster.

Hamsters become nervous when they are held in a cupped hand. So hold your pet by gently grasping the loose skin on the back of its neck while your other hand is under it. Never pick it up by just the neck, and always keep your hand under it.

Ferrets should be picked up using two hands. One of your hands should support its chest, and the other should support its hips.

Ferrets should be picked up with two hands.

The chest-to-chest hold is a safe way to carry your rabbit.

Preventing Problems

Because of their friendly nature, gerbils do not usually bite. They enjoy being handled. In fact, the more you handle them, the better they like people. To pick up a gerbil, scoop it onto your open palm. You also can pick it up by the base of the tail. Do not pick it up by the tip of the tail because that part is very fragile.

When handling a guinea pig, never pick it up by its scruff, which is the hair on its neck. Gently cradle your guinea pig in one hand while securing its body with the other hand.

Learning to lift your rabbit requires time and patience. One thing to keep in mind is that you must always hold your rabbit snugly against your body. One safe way to hold a rabbit is called the "chest-to-chest" hold. This means carrying the rabbit vertically (up and down) against your chest with its head near yours. Another way to carry it is called the "football hold." This means holding the rabbit with its rump in one of your hands and its head in the crook, or bend, of your elbow.

Chapter 7
You and Your New Pet

A dwarf rabbit

After you bring a small mammal into your home, you will be happy to spend time with it. You can learn more about your pet by logging onto the Internet, with an adult's permission. There, you will find a lot of information. You might also want to join a "virtual community" of others your age who have the same kind of pet.

Keep loving and learning more about your pet. Then you and your mouse, rat, hamster, gerbil, guinea pig, rabbit, or ferret can spend many happy, fun-filled years together.

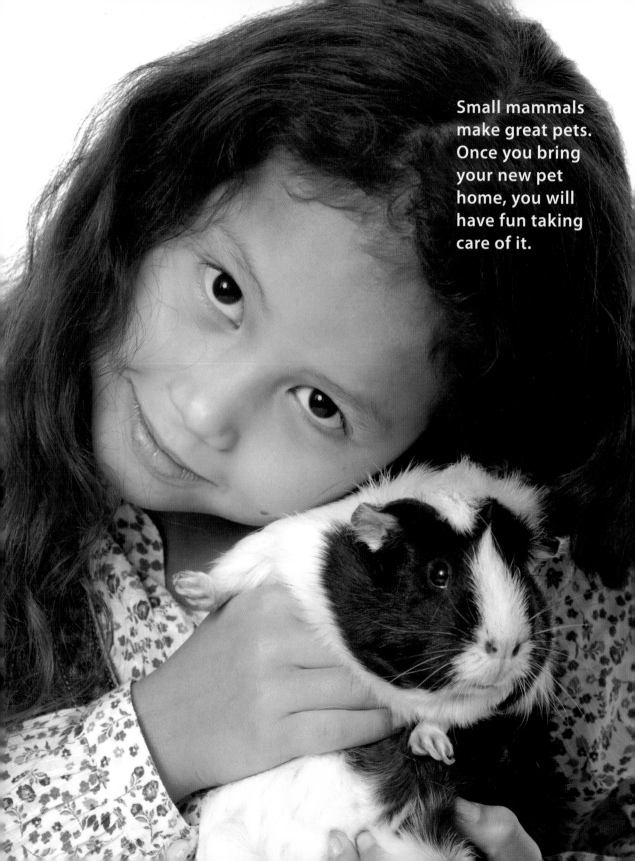

Small mammals make great pets. Once you bring your new pet home, you will have fun taking care of it.

Life Cycle of a Hamster

1. When hamsters are born, their eyes are closed, and they do not have any hair.

2. After a few weeks, baby hamsters begin to grow hair, and their eyes start to open.

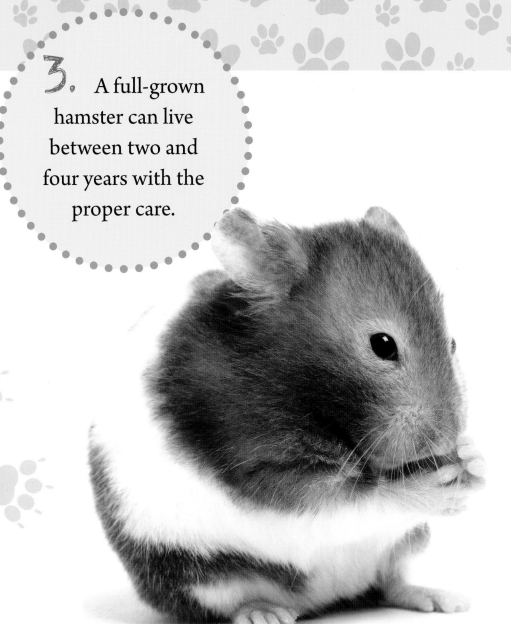

3. A full-grown hamster can live between two and four years with the proper care.

Words to Know

burrow—To dig a hole or a tunnel in bedding and hide in it.

galvanized—Made of a metal specially coated to prevent rust.

hoard—To hide food to eat at a later time.

lethargic—Sleepy, without energy.

mammals—Warm-blooded animals whose babies feed on their mothers' milk.

neuter—To operate on a male animal so that it cannot reproduce. This operation prevents overpopulation.

parasite—A tiny animal that lives inside another bigger animal and makes it sick.

sisal—A strong fiber used to make rope and other items.

spay—To operate on a female animal so that it cannot reproduce. This operation prevents overpopulation.

Read More About Small Mammals

Books

Bearce, Stephanie. *Care for a Pet Guinea Pig*. Hockessin, Del.: Mitchell Lane Publishers, 2009.

Kawa, Katie. *Cuddly Rabbits*. New York: Gareth Stevens Publishing, 2011.

McNicholas, June. *Rats*. Chicago, Ill.: Heinemann Library, 2010.

Internet Addresses

American Humane Association
 <http://www.americanhumane.org/>

ASPCA Kids: Pet Care
 <http://www.aspca.org/Home/ASPCAKids/
 Pet-Care.aspx>

Index